Great African-Americans

Booker T.
WASHINGTON

by Riley Flynn   Consulting Editor: Gail Saunders-Smith, PhD

CAPSTONE PRESS
a capstone imprint

Pebble Books are published by Capstone Press,
1710 Roe Crest Drive, North Mankato, Minnesota 56003
www.capstonepub.com

Library of Congress Cataloging-in-Publication Data
Flynn, Riley.
  Booker T. Washington / by Riley Flynn.
     pages cm.—(Pebble books. Great African-Americans)
  Summary: "Simple text and photographs present the life of Booker T. Washington"—Provided
by publisher.
  Includes bibliographical references and index.
  ISBN 978-1-4765-3952-2 (library binding)
  ISBN 978-1-4765-5156-2 (paperback)
  ISBN 978-1-4765-6013-7 (ebook pdf)
  1. Washington, Booker T., 1856–1915—Juvenile literature. 2. African Americans—Biography—
Juvenile literature. 3. Educators—United States—Biography—Juvenile literature. I. Title.
  E185.97.W4F55 2014
  370.92—dc23
  [B]   2013035321

Editorial Credits
Erika L. Shores, editor; Ashlee Suker, designer; Wanda Winch, media researcher;
Laura Manthe, production specialist

Photo Credits
The Historic New Orleans Collection: Williams Research Center, cover; Library of Congress:
Prints and Photographs Division, 4, 10, 12, 14, 20; Royal Photo Co. "The National Negro
Business League Louisville, Ky., August 18, 1909." An Era of progress and promise: The Clifton
Conference. Priscilla Pub. Co. 1910. p.413. http://digital.ncdcr.gov/cdm/ref/collection/
p249901coll37/id/4566, 16; Shutterstock: Urfin, books design; Tuskegee University
Archives, 6, 8, 18

Note to Parents and Teachers

The Great African-Americans set supports national curriculum standards for
social studies related to people, places, and environments. This book describes
and illustrates Booker T. Washington. The images support early readers in
understanding the text. The repetition of words and phrases helps early readers
learn new words. This book also introduces early readers to subject-specific
vocabulary words, which are defined in the Glossary section. Early readers may
need assistance to read some words and to use the Table of Contents, Glossary,
Read More, Internet Sites, and Index sections of the book.

Printed in the United States of America in North Mankato, Minnesota.
092013   007764CGS14

Table of Contents

Meet Booker

Booker T. Washington was a teacher, speaker, and leader. Booker helped start a school for African-Americans. He became one of the most respected African-American men in the world.

*Booker
around 1872*

1856

born

Young Booker

Booker was born on a farm in Virginia in 1856. He did not have a last name because he was born a slave. As a young boy, Booker did yard work. He also carried water to field-workers.

Booker's family home in West Virginia

1856

born

1865

moves to West Virginia

When Booker was 9, the Civil War (1861–1865) ended, and slaves were freed. Booker and his family traveled to West Virginia.

Booker worked in a salt mine.

But he wanted to go to school.

A Hampton Institute classroom

1856
born

1865
moves to
West Virginia

1872
goes to
Hampton
Institute

Soon a school for black children opened nearby. Booker needed a last name at school. He chose the name Washington. In 1872 Booker left home to study at Hampton Institute in Virginia.

Booker, front row, with Tuskegee teachers

1856
born

1865
moves to
West Virginia

1872
goes to
Hampton
Institute

1875
graduates
from Hampton
Institute

1881
begins
teaching at
Tuskegee

As an Adult

Booker graduated in 1875. He became a teacher. In 1881 he founded a new school for African-Americans called Tuskegee Institute. Booker wanted his students to learn useful skills at this school.

Booker speaking in 1910

1856 born

1865 moves to West Virginia

1872 goes to Hampton Institute

1875 graduates from Hampton Institute

1881 begins teaching at Tuskegee

Booker believed African-Americans would gain respect by working hard. In 1895 Booker gave a famous speech in Atlanta, Georgia. He talked about his ideas for how white people and African-Americans could work together.

1895

gives famous
speech in Atlanta,
Georgia

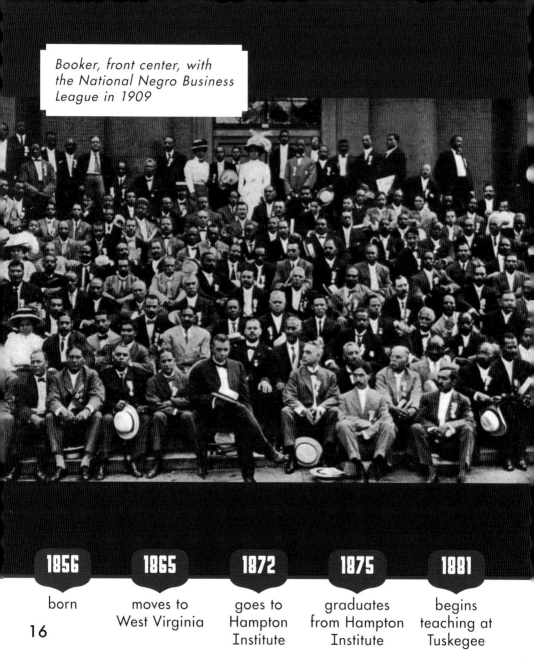

Booker, front center, with the National Negro Business League in 1909

1856	**1865**	**1872**	**1875**	**1881**
born	moves to West Virginia	goes to Hampton Institute	graduates from Hampton Institute	begins teaching at Tuskegee

Later Years

After his speech Booker was asked to speak all over the country. He became a spokesperson for African-Americans. In 1900 Booker helped start the National Negro Business League. He wanted to teach African-Americans about business.

1895

gives famous speech in Atlanta, Georgia

1900

starts business league

1856	1865	1872	1875	1881
born	moves to West Virginia	goes to Hampton Institute	graduates from Hampton Institute	begins teaching at Tuskegee

In 1901 Booker wrote a book

called *Up from Slavery*.

He wrote about his life and ideas.

Booker worked hard to

educate and inspire others.

1895
gives famous
speech in Atlanta,
Georgia

1900
starts business
league

1901
writes book

| 1856 | 1865 | 1872 | 1875 | 1881 |

born

moves to
West Virginia

goes to
Hampton
Institute

graduates
from Hampton
Institute

begins
teaching at
Tuskegee

20

| **1856** | **1865** | **1872** | **1875** | **1881** |

born

moves to
West Virginia

goes to
Hampton
Institute

graduates
from Hampton
Institute

begins
teaching at
Tuskegee

Booker died in 1915. He is famous for starting Tuskegee Institute. He changed lives through the power of education. People remember him as a leader in the African-American community.

1895
gives famous speech in Atlanta, Georgia

1900
starts business league

1901
writes book

1915
dies at age 59

Glossary

Civil War—the U.S. war fought between the Northern states and the Southern states; the Civil War lasted from 1861–1865

community—a group of people who live in the same area or have something in common

found—to set up or start something such as a school or town

graduate—to finish all required classes at a school

inspire—to influence or encourage other people in a good way

mine—an underground supply of minerals, metals, coal, or salt

respect—to admire and have a good opinion of someone

slave—a person who is owned by another person; slaves are not free to choose their homes or jobs

Read More

Dunn, Joeming. *Booker T. Washington.* Bio-Graphics. Edina, Minn.: Magic Wagon, 2009.

McKissack, Patricia, and Fredrick. *Booker T. Washington: African-American Leader.* Famous African Americans. Berkeley Heights, N.J.: Enslow Elementary, 2013.

Slade, Suzanne. *Booker T. Washington: Teacher, Speaker, and Leader.* Biographies. Minneapolis: Picture Window Books, 2008.

Internet Sites

FactHound offers a safe, fun way to find Internet sites related to this book. All of the sites on FactHound have been researched by our staff.

Here's all you do:
Visit *www.facthound.com*
Type in this code: 9781476539522

Super-cool stuff!

Check out projects, games and lots more at
www.capstonekids.com

Critical Thinking Using the Common Core

1. Booker was respected for his work in the African-American community. What does it mean to be respected? (Key Ideas and Details)

2. What did Booker do to help African-Americans get an education and learn about business? How do you think he helped African-Americans work with white people? (Integration of Knowledge and Ideas)

Index

Word Count: 285
Grade: 1
Early-Intervention Level: 22

24